Borko Jovanovic

MEMORIES
OF TUESDAY

Poems

(1984-2017)

CONTENTS

Embracing Emptiness

"Each poet is an unhappy lover and every unhappy lover wants to tell his story..."

Morning in a Motel

As I was urinating
in the bathroom of this small motel
in woods of Massachusetts
suddenly and finally
I faced man in the mirror

He was middle-aged
with rings of night about his eyes
a lone man, awakened in a foreign land
holding something in his left hand

Patiently
I accepted this absurd encounter
and keeping an eye on the stranger
flushed the toilet

Chill

Autumn chill is in the air

Aimless, restless, you pace
through nervous silence of sunlit rooms
and hesitant stop
and open a book and shut it
and pace again
with hands over your face

Chill of autumn
slides a dagger
into summer's
sweet content

On the Beach

Oh richness of the world

Six PM tide closing in
blue and white and the wind
my lungs full of rich humid space

Sun
beaming a red song
for end of the day
Children, lovers, souls hover
busy daydreaming

Pleasures of the beach
thighs shoulders
well oiled all
seemingly pleased
with things as they are

Waves, waves, waves and wind
infinitely reflecting the red song

While I celebrate this richness
this emptiness
this miraculous absence of pain

Borges

All things in this room

Colors of dagger at dawn
pale blue space of Arizona
Magic life of chess-pieces
Babylon lottery

Unfathomable algebra
of a woman's smile

Children we never had
abandoned children that we are

Unbearable richness of world
unbearable emptiness

And yet
in small towns on Sundays
all is well as people take their walk
women eat ice-cream, men smoke

A giant golden tiger
runs softly along Route 91
seeking an opponent
who can best him in being nowhere

An old man, alone
in this room and everywhere

Open

It was a pleasant evening
in the coffeehouse
The four of us discussed
questions of dimensions, perception
liberation and time

And we agreed that nothingness
must be thought of
in order to be spoken of

As we fell silent
I found pleasure in the thought
that long ago I was spoken for
by nothingness

Later, as I sat facing
still life of furniture
I envisioned
the four of us philosophers
as four coffee cups

each in his corner of a table
immovable
and open from above

Piece on Magritte

Window after window after window
beyond each one
a woman a man a flower a sky

In endless procession
unexpected images
of ordinary things
acquainting themselves
with their one infinite name

Tears

As I was watching a late night film
etherized in the armchair

it suddenly occurred to me
that in order
to see the face of God
one must be able
to altogether give up the world

And as I switched off the TV set
in that instant

I thought I caught a glimpse
of meaning of the Fall

Kernel

Trust not my words
song is vanity

But we do have a common cause

Otherwise your mind and mine
would have never met
in patient darkness beyond eyelids

And tell me
can you hear black on white
can you see the never-ending murmur

Just there in that sweet kernel
eternal silent hum

Letters to a Kind Gatekeeper

for Tetsuji Murakami (1927-1987)

"O venerable Master! You (indeed) have great compassion.
Your grace exceeds that of my parents.
Had you then disclosed to me (the truth)
How could this today have happened to me."

Experience

Maitre
I have something
to report today

I touched the sun
you taught me
how to play with

Now I am barely alive

Please
tell me what to do

I kneel before you
forehead and palms
flat on the floor

Facing

Upon receiving the news
of your illness
I've sat here for a long time
breathing from the pit of my stomach

My left fist
rests on my left knee
holding the key
which I received from you

My right hand
is holding a pen
expressing sorrow
which comes from nowhere
and goes nowhere

In this moment of silence
there is no difference
between you and me
as I sit here facing nothing

And I bow my head before you
in gratitude
as tears keep rolling down my face

By the Pond

Sitting here by the pond
water surface clam and clear

Great void
and nothing else

Birds moving down south
cool of the night
soothing my heart

In my fist
memory of you

Abode

One year and one month
since you passed away

Today
I don't remember
anything you taught me

Just watching snow
come and go

Fists
useless on my knees

My heart wide open

I thought
it would please you to know
this is were you abide

Coming of Age

Now that you are gone
I feel your presence all the time

Yesterday
in the middle of a supermarket
from behind a fruit stand
you attacked me

A long punch first
a turn and then a kick

I reacted naturally
just as you have taught me:
a block a turn another block
silence

And as you vanished back
into the neon light
I thought that I saw
that smile of yours

Then I bent over
to pick up some oranges
and none knew
I was bowing to you

I walk freely now
as I have no place to hide

Hum

Things I used to talk about
do not exist

I walk
and everything I pass
disappears

I've opened my palms
to welcome the oncoming illusions

There is no difference
between them and myself

And I can't tell
if I hum this song for you
or you hum it for me

On the Road

Years have gone by
and yet in my heart

boundless moment
of our meeting hums still

A lone man
with fistful of nothing
I am always in good company

Walking the avenues
of one city after another

I show you places
you've never seen

Love of Love

"Trip no further pretty sweeting
Journeys end in lovers meeting..."

Thinking of You

How sweet it is to think of you

All evening I've been reading
about Prayer of the Heart

With the nameless old pilgrim
I traveled
three thousand vrstas
through Siberian woods
and thirty-nine light-years
through my own heart

I haven't arrived anywhere

Just ended up on my bed
thinking of you

Sunset

Traveling by car through dark woods
a bleeding sunset green lawn
and winding back roads
of small white towns of Massachusetts

It's here again: a racing heartbeat
a moaning ball of lead
exploding into space

A terrible thing happened to us
somewhere, some time ago
and I knew nothing of it

And you
you are three thousand miles away
and it'll be months until I see you again

Screaming sunset dark woods
road after road after road
a moan none can hear

Back Pain

As I was trying
to drown pain in my back
as the last immovable customer
on this red and orange patio
inhaling
sweet summer wind of midnight

It suddenly occurred to me
that this pain would vanish
should I forgive myself
my love for you

And I allowed myself
to love you
as I limped back to the car
and later
crucified on my bed
I uttered words never spoken before:

Oh my love
why have thy forsaken me?

And as all things
sunk into primordial void
it felt as if
someone was watching both of us
with infinite sadness, infinite pity

Tongue in Cheek

Yes it was nice of you
to ask me upstairs for a drink
and then hours later
we lie naked under covers

your cats purring on top of me
and we are one happy family
all piled up, legs, arms intertwined

generating light
that illuminates
this cool spring night until dawn

My tongue in your cheek
in your eyes
in your beaming face
revealing unspeakable

Hounds of Winter

January's
cruel month to fall apart:
(this mad naked frozen innocence
chained to a peasant cart)

You left
claiming my lack of flexibility
abundance of old fashion
and that I lectured much
pointing finger at you

This was true love
someone whispers
watching white walls wink

Thoughts conceived
in dead winter midnight:
doorway to the end of logic

In a place without light
the howling hounds of your absence
eat my live heart

Love of Love

Yes I love love
the love of eyes
and the love of flesh
and that mad holy glow
when in darkness
two bodies clash

It is lack of courage
that brings me here

If I could walk away
and let this game pass me by
I could turn attention inward
toward the heart
and finally face the glow inside

Yes this love of love
points to a place
where in light itself
rests that real face

Song's Caress

I am very happy here
writing songs alone at night

For world outside
I care less and less

Drinking wine and humming inside
feels like a sweet secret caress
under the dinner table

As if
we've just fooled
all other guests

Cup of Light

for Svetlana Lunt

Shortcut

"If I have told you of earthly things
and ye believe not, how shall ye believe
if I tell you of heavenly things?"

Walking along the beach with you
my heart is at peace

World is right: earth, water, air
cool moon fire

Gulls don't cry at night
but I hear them:
night will change into day
light will come, gulls will cry
waves will wash this past

I accept it all
cries unheard
the unfathomable algebra of now

You are walking by my side
leading quietly
along a magic shortcut
through my bleeding wanderings

In this luminous presence
heart is at peace
not wondering why

Summer Stored

Ah this early summer day

Buzzing bees, white clouds
Sun beaming a golden song

I inhaled one whole white cloud
and some golden dust from your brow
and promised myself to keep them stored
until December
or January
or February

Gift

Four more hours
and I'll see you again

Amidst shop windows
and shadows in business suits
I laugh aloud at such foolishness

And then in secret
put palms together
in gratitude for such a gift

A Good Evening

What an evening we've had

You were away
visiting with your family and friends
and I've spent my time downtown
drinking and thinking of you

Ah when you return
there will be so much to tell

Another World

I woke up early this morning
my heart madly
living on its own

Last night I learned
of your plan to depart
and at dawn fell asleep
into a long sequence
of rainy November mornings

in each of which, staff in hand
I walk along a country road

Through the fields dark and heavy
a half-tame lame wolf
follows along
howling into the mists
his protection song

I keep my eyes on the road
and murmur a prayer
from another world

Naked

And ah oh so swiftly
you swept me off my feet

and turned back
 to your long-distance lover
of three-and-a-half years

"I've invested so much of my being
in that relationship" you said

In merciless light
of an early September morning
I sit naked on my bed

and vaguely sense the horror
and unbearable lightness
of having nothing at all

Cup of Light

"I have meat to eat that ye know not of..."

It is late at night
and I drink this cup of wine
grateful for my good fortune

When I fall asleep
perhaps you will come to me again

and wishing not to betray your lover
hand me quickly
a cup of light from your heart

Yes when I fall asleep
I will lay this body down
and walk the path
where only light matters

Strange

This love is
sharp as a blade

We've only touched
and look I am bleeding

I lick the wound
and taste a mystery
ah so dark and deep

Marina Postcards

"My father wrote beautifully, Esme' *interrupted.*
I'm saving a number of his letters for posterity".

Trinity

for Mirko Dobrijevic

Heart is a fool on the left
World is a wound on the right

I kneel in between
head on the ground

The sword never comes

Tin Fall

for Patricia Munoz

Autumn winds
are the Summer's Fall

Each seed bears fruit
and after celebration
cold sets in

Past jubilations
echo like tin

Methamaticks

for William Baxter

Deep winter snow
solitary walks
music and mathematics

A natural dwelling:
this useless purity of mind

And yes we do know well
there is nothing to find

Mind seeks a labyrinth
to forget the fall of heart

Meeting

for K.M.

Eyes shut
I kissed your wound
and then my wound
you swiftly revealed

Now I kiss
white walls of Winter
skin of these lips
neatly peeled

Good kisses are red
and my face is blue

Marina

for Martha Drayton

Ray Ban (your Western man)
well trimmed and tan
observes the Ocean
with no emotion

With subtle caution
he plays with notion
of end of motion

(A very fine suit
nothing to shoot
no place to go
nothing to know)

Here's your man
well dressed and tan

staring at the end
of water and land

In the End

for Robert Moorhead

This is what I want:
a clear day, sailboats, breeze

to write it down, and kneel
hands on knees

Resist temptation of rhyme:
clear day, bay, sailboats on the way
to some place and back

Like a sack of potatoes:
immovable on the beach
mother water, father sky
not wondering which or why
or what

And this is how I'll go
into the storm's eye:
kneeling in sand, blink twice:
good-bye, good-bye
good-bye

Big Sur

"Before the game

One shuts one eye
Peeks into every corner of self
Checks for nails for thieves
For cuckoo eggs

One shuts the other eye
Squats and jumps
Jumps high high high
To the top of oneself

From the top one falls
Falls deep deep deep
To the bottom of one's abyss

Whoever does not fall apart
Whoever remains whole
And stands up whole
He can play"

Green Street

I walked all night
mocking moonlight
along some steep streets
calling for a fall

At dawn
facing a wall
I saw I was innocent

From behind the rim
of a coffee cup
there it is

end of a world

Big Ocean-Sky

Big ocean-sky
and nowhere to go West

A lifetime spent
to get this far

and lo!

Here's an old man
smoking a cigar

drumming a tune
on the roof
of a rented car

Sunset

I ate
that rhubarb pie of sky

and drank
ink blue wine
that smelled of pine

Then I laid my head
on a caramel hill

and as a well fed man
embraced evening chill

Fog

Fog rolls in
and eats the world

On the flute
made of a bone
of my old teacher
I play a hollow note
for that dead madman

No shadows
to hang on to

Wine before me
fog in my eyes

Apart

Dead decaying remains
of awesome ocean monsters
algae, flies

An endless day
spent in aimless wandering
at this final destination

Sun sets and you stand
in mother-water
world above
world below

At distance
caramel hills
in light that remains

And you are
neither apart
nor a part of it

Major Bear

Seven teasers
above the hill

seven jokers
to set the bill

Four and three
I bow to Thee

Do re
mi fa

sol
la
ti

Campsite

From afar
beyond their fires
tourists, half asleep
talking night talk

Children in tents
dreaming of a swim
in the Big Sur River

A dream come true

I inhale
cold air full of stars

and shed seven tears
for the man left behind

A Year from Last Tuesday

Lay of the Land

Something happened
In my long travelling dream

I woke up
In this mediocre place

Everything planned
Turned out half-done

And now
Bed, table, clock
Window and a tree
Coffee

Maybe that's it
Where I was going
All along

Poetry

From the beginning
Life was a nightmare

But language
And word games
Provided some joy

It was all deeply felt
And rung true

We called it Poetry

But then
Who knows what it was

Travel

Now it seems

Any place is good enough
If you look at it
From where you are

But all those travelogues and poems
In my secret drawer

Who wrote them?

Projections

First, the World

Then you understood
It was a projection
Of something

That projection after a while
Became projection
Of something else

And so on and on

Who knows who
Is in the play here?
I wanted to ask

But now
We are almost out of time

It all Happened

It all happened
Lasted a while
And it was fine

Lessons were learnt

Then we moved on
To another state
And none there cared
For personal history

Some photographs
Do remain
In tin box under the bed

Cycling

Even if I remember the past
I may just have to repeat it?

If this is
The only game in town
I am leaving Dodge City

But wait

I might have been here before

Sleep Dance
for LVD

I turn left
you turn left

You turn right
and I follow

Two heads
on one pillow
four legs and arms
moving as one

And so slowly we dance
steps measured
by the all-wise breath of night

In speechless agreement
across stardust we glide so
into the morning

Postscript (circa 1998-2000)

"*Embracing Emptiness*" deals with the frustration with and the acceptance of an empty internal space and lack of direction. The first version of poem "*Chill*" I wrote in 1987 at the South Street apartment in Northampton, Massachusetts. It was a very large, top floor apartment, with light coming in from three sides. I was very lonely there, although the view and sunlight were quite delightful. This sense of desperate loneliness in the presence of beauty is hard to describe. "*Happiness*" I wrote circa 1992 in Evanston, Illinois. "*Borges*" was envisioned in Otis, Massachusetts, in a large sunny kitchen, on Cold Spring Farm, in 1985 or 1986, and written in various forms years later. I read much of J.L. Borges when I was young, and his way of thinking affected me quite a bit. I have struggled with this poem more than with any other, probably because one-page limit I impose upon myself if not enough to cover the topic, and a "Cantos" type of production may be the only way to go. "*Morning in a Motel*" was experienced in a motel in Northampton in 1991 or 1992, during one of my nostalgic visits to the area.

"*Open*" was written after an evening in coffeehouse on Dempster Street in Evanston, and was originally dedicated to Robert

Moorhead, who was present. Many such dedications I decided to drop from book's final version, and to keep only those in the "Marina Postcards" section. "Piece on Magritte" was written in the coffeehouse on Main Street and Hinman in Evanston, after the Magritte Chicago exhibit. "Tears" was written in the basement of the house on Forest Avenue, in Evanston, after the fact, circa 1992, and followed some intense readings of the New Testament in the woods of Massachusetts.

"Letters to a Kind Gatekeeper" presents the mourning process prompted by the sudden illness and death of my teacher, Tetsuji Murakami. Gatekeeper in this context is one who stands at the gate of truth or liberation or shows the way. The Gateless Gate is a well-known collection of Zen koans, and I took the idea for the title from there. These poems were written between 1986 and 1992. *"Facing"* was written first, as I sat on the floor of the apartment on Fort Hill Terrace in Northampton, while my wife at that time, was reading in the bedroom. Other poems followed, and they are probably the most sincere ones I wrote. This was an intense period, when many things happened and all my beliefs were challenged. In addition, my health declined and I developed a lower back pain, which persisted for several years.

"*Experience*" describes the unleashing of some of the powers inherent in all of us. These events caught me by surprise, putting my alleged "knowledge" at the time in proper perspective. "*By the Pond*" and "*Abode*" are really love poems for the guru. Both were written in Amherst, Massachusetts, the first one at Puffer's Pond. "*Coming of Age*" was written after a visit to a supermarket "Stop and Shop" in Hadley, Massachusetts, when I realized that I had no place to go and no place to hide from whatever was to happen to me. It brings about a topic from (as I understand it) Guru Yoga, in which one envisions one's guru at all times, even sitting on one's shoulder. Thus, the Guru participates in everything that happens.

"*Love of Love*" was completed in 1995. Unfortunately, my so-called "love life" at the time has been all but a holiday. Part of my view on this subject matter is spelled out in "Love of Love". "*Sunset*" was rewritten many times and experienced in 1987 during a drive from Logan airport to Western Massachusetts, and I wrote it for my former wife. "*Hounds of Winter*" was written in January and February 1996, inspired in part by an album by Sting entitled "Mercury Falling", and in particular by the song "Hounds of Winter". In the process of writing this poem, which had many versions, my weight dropped by twenty pounds, which translates to about a pound per line. *"Thinking of You"* was written in 1991, in Evanston, for a young woman who inspired me to write the section "Cup of Light". *"Song's Caress"* was written in the kitchen of the house on Forest Avenue, in Evanston, in 1992. I recall being very happy after putting it on paper.

"Cup of Light" was written in 1991 and 1992 for a young woman I had romantic feelings for, and spent much time with for about a year ("Svetlana Lunt"). Not much happened between us, and although some poems reflect pain, I feel good when I read them. The entire experience, I am happy to say, had a good impact on me.

"Marina Postcards" consists of short messages to my friends, whom I chose to name in this section. The Marina is a neighborhood of San Francisco. Each poem refers to a conversation. An exception is the poem *"Meeting"* which I wrote for the same person I wrote *"Hounds of Winter"* for. I like this poem quite a bit. It reminds me of the French film "Pierrot the Fool" with Jean-Paul Belmondo (circa 1970) in which, prior to his death, the main protagonist paints his face bright blue. It also (perhaps much too obviously) has elements of the well-known song "Roses are

red, violets are blue, sugar is sweet, but not as sweet as you".

"*Big Sur*" brings about some sort of conclusion to this early undertaking. I wrote it after a trip to Northern California in 1994. I visited there in 1996 as well, and some poems from the "*Marina*" section also followed. In "*Big Ocean-Sky*" I am an old man who has finished his travels. In "*Sunset*" I describe the tactile sense of the landscape of the area. In "*Fog*" I pay tribute to my late teacher and to the past. Green Street is in San Francisco, and I actually walked all over town one night and saw some strange things. Some days later, I swam (stood) in the Big Sur River, and did look at the sky for what seemed a long time. Poem "*Major Bear*" refers to observing the night sky and to the teachings provided by the Russian mystic Gourdjieff. Strangely enough, during this trip I witnessed a meeting of a group in "Work" as it is called, in a coffeehouse in the Marina.

If I may make a general statement, I'd say the value of poetry is in revealing what is hidden. It provides all involved and interested parties with a taste of greater forces, which are much too close to home to be seen in so-called ordinary ways. There are, of course, other ways of dealing with such forces, but that is a different matter all-together. With not much left to say at this point, I leave you, my kind and patient reader, right here where you are.

Postscript 2018

This entire book *"Memories of Tuesday"* is
homage to poems I have written over the
years. The previous version was entitled
"Chill" and appeared in a couple of versions
circa 1998-2002, in Chicago.

Poems in the last section, *"A Year from Last
Tuesday,"* have been written relatively recently.
After a certain point, explaining what was said
and why and when, becomes less interesting.
It is just life that happens. Samuel Beckett's
"Krapp's Last Tape" comes to mind.

References

"Each poet is an unhappy lover..." is quoted from
"The Black Prince" by Iris Murdoch. *Poem by
Chi Hsien (Hsiang Yen) in praise of his master Kuei
Shan* is quoted from "Chan and Zen
Teachings" Vol. I, by Charles Luk. *"Trip no
further pretty sweeting ..."* is quoted from a short
poem by William Shakespeare. *"If I have told you
of earthly things ..."* is from the Gospel by John
(3:12), and *"I have meat to eat that ye know not of"*
is from John (4:32). *"My father wrote beautifully,
Esme' interrupted..."* is from "For Esme'-with
Love and Squalor" by J.D. Salinger. *"Before the
Game"* is a poem by Vasko Popa, in my own
translation from Serbian. Needless to say, all
errors are mine.